Pearlie...

I Dream

Peace In The Home

Written by Yvonne Bardwell Cox   Illustrations by Stacy Johnson

AuthorHouse™
1663 Liberty Drive
Bloomington, IN 47403
www.authorhouse.com
Phone: 833-262-8899

This book is printed on acid-free paper.

ISBN: 978-1-6655-4718-5 (sc)
ISBN: 978-1-6655-4717-8(e)

Library of Congress Control Number: 2021924860

Print information available on the last page.

Published by AuthorHouse 01/12/2022

authorHOUSE

"Commit thy works unto the Lord, and thy thoughts shall be established."
Proverbs 16:3

Acknowledgements

The thought of writing children's books has pondered my inner mind for many years. From my childhood, throughout my young adult life, I have always had a sincere love and interest to work with children with special needs. I am fortunate to have experienced and to have been offered education positions requiring teaching children with and without disabilities. Yes, I am a true Educator. Throughout my teaching career, I would often imagine different scenarios related to my childhood memories. My imagination has always been broad, yet creative and detailed. Now I am retired and still at work for children, but the Lord has instilled the books in my mind and heart that He wants me to put on paper.

I am eternally grateful to my grandmama Pearl Moore Bardwell, to whom Pearlie is named. She taught us the Word of God at night in front of a small space heater. I remember the day she taught me the Lord's Prayer. To my mother, my mama, and my friend Hattie Bardwell Pace. I love you to the moon and back. Thank you for loving and taking care of me throughout my sicknesses that I did not understand the severity of. I am truly here because of you.

I am thankful for my husband, Pastor Tommy L. Cox, for his continuous encouragement and Godly wisdom and advice. I am very grateful for my son, Michael Kelly Johnson, and my daughter-in-law Stacy Johnson who have helped to make the "Pearlie...I Dream" series come to life. The both of you are truly a team of knowledge and creative minds. Michael joined me in editing and handling all legalities and Stacy's ability to edit and create mind-blowing illustrations, our triangle is complete. A special thank you to Mrs. Mable Young, for confidentially reading/editing my books and offering positive comments, when I was so reluctant to ask anyone to read what I had written.

I am sincerely grateful for this opportunity to become an Author of Children Books.

Dedication

I would like to dedicate this book series in memory of my family members who are resting in the arms of the Lord. Thank you for beautiful memories of a lifetime.

- My grandmother, Mrs. Pearl (Grandma Pearl) Moore Bardwell (in loving memory)

- My mother, Mrs. Hattie (Mama Hattie) Bardwell Pace

- My aunt, Mrs. Martha (Auntie Martha) Bardwell Bishop (in loving memory)

- My brother, Randolph (Doc) Bardwell (in loving memory)

- My brother, Douglas (Doug) Bardwell

- My brother, Steven (Steve) Bardwell

- My sister, Patricia Ann (Tennie) Bardwell Collier

- My sister/niece, Tonda (Lil T) Bardwell Fleming

- My first cousin, Julius (Ju Ju) Bardwell

- My first cousin, Tommy Lee Bardwell Fort (in loving memory)

This book series is entitled Pearlie ... I Dream. Each book is about a day in the life of Pearlie. A little girl growing up in a small town with a big loving family. The first "Pearlie ... I Dream" book is "Peace in the Home." This book sets the stage for future books to follow all the unique adventures Pearlie experienced. How the love of family builds you into the person you want to become and to believe in yourself!

Hello, my name is Pearlie. I was named after my Grandma Pearl. I am sure this is because I might look like her or even have her ways. I really do not know the real reason. All I know is, I love my name. I am so happy to be her namesake.

When she spoke, I listened. She taught me the "Lord's Prayer." I remembered every word she said.

At first, I did not believe in myself. Then things in my life began to happen. Slowly but surely, I had a change of mind. Sometimes I would daydream and then I would dream when I was fast asleep. Whatever I started out to do – would come to life because I BELIEVED it would happen!

All things are possible – if you only believe!

5

When you look at me, you will see a little dark-skinned girl with as much hair as body. They have always said, "Pearlie you have a head full of hair." Some people call me Tennie Weenie, I guess that is because of my size. My brothers call me Mickey, they say I look like a little mouse with my two big hair puffs.

One thing you will remember about me is I am wearing a big smile as bright as the summer sun at noonday.

Why is my smile so big? I am happy all the time … because Grandma Pearl teaches us to think happy thoughts. She says, "When you think good stuff, good stuff will happen for you."

9

At night, before I go to sleep, I always say my prayers. I do not count sheep; I think of good stuff. After I go to sleep, my mind carries me to some places. Some I have been before and some I have not. My dreams are so clear, and I can see the bright colors of the rainbow. They are so close I can touch them.

11

In my dreams, I can go wherever I want to go and return home safely. But this time, I am doing what I thought I could not do. I am flying as if I have the wings of an angel. I am looking down at our home. I see my family. I am dreaming and I know what I am doing and how to do it. All I have to do is believe!

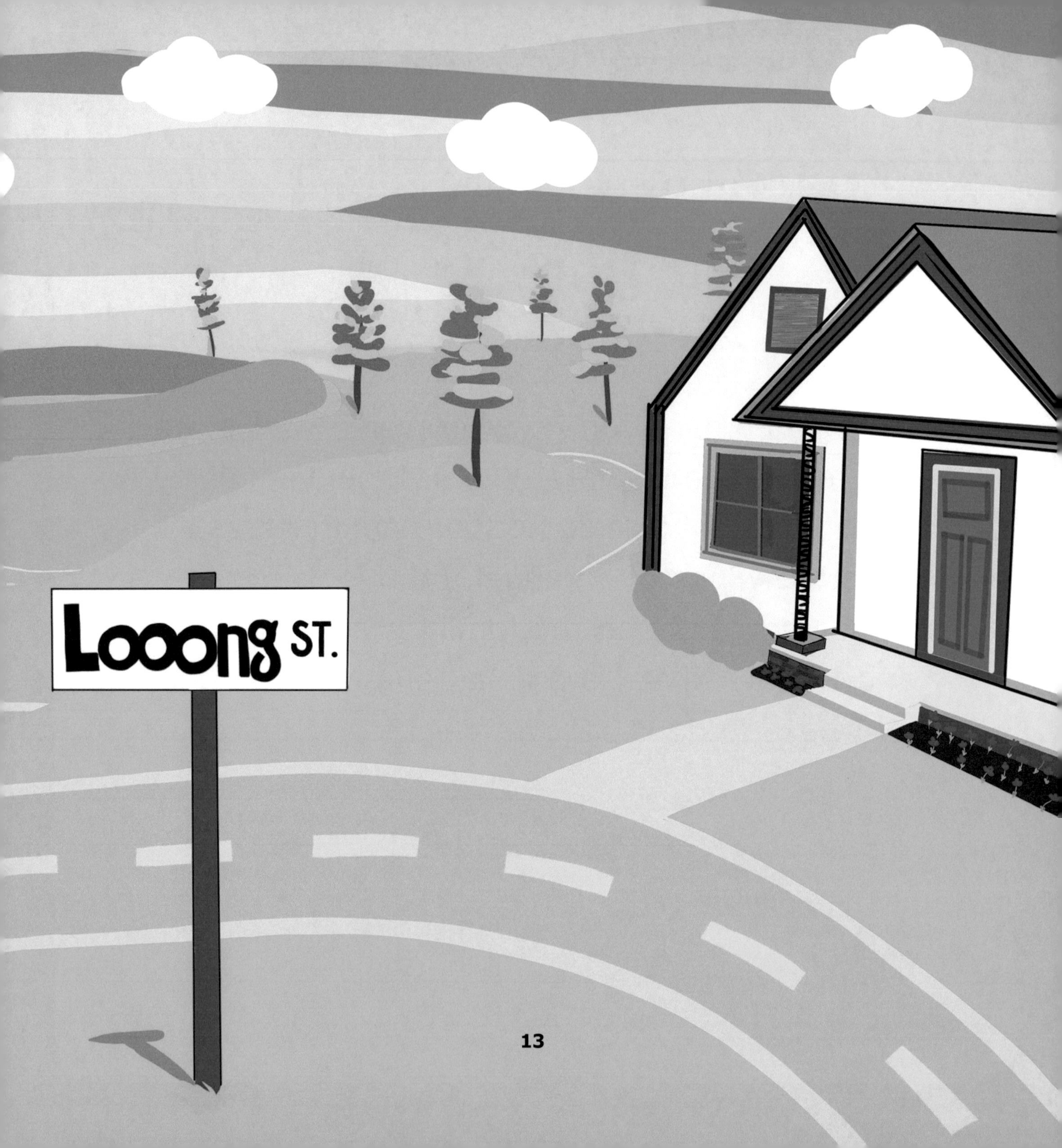
Looong ST.

I grew up in a very different kind of way. Today, I am at home. My family and I live in the small town of Starkville, Mississippi. Down the road and around the curves on a very long street, called Long Street. We live in a white house with a screen door and a big front porch. Our home is not too big, but not too small, exactly right for all of us.

Meet my family. I live with my Mama Hattie, Grandma Pearl, Auntie Martha, three brothers (Doc, Doug, and Steve), one sister (Tennie), one niece (Little T, she is just like my little sister) and two first cousins (Tommy Lee and Ju Ju). Where do I fit in? I do not know. But they tell me I am the knee baby, the middle child.

17

We call my mama, Mama Hattie. She is a pretty lady to me. She has silky black hair, and she smiles as I do. Mama Hattie goes to work early in the morning. She comes home late in the evening when the sun is going down. She loves and takes care of all of us, her family.

19

I love it when she is at home and has time to wash, press, and comb my hair. She likes to give me two ponytails. When she does, it makes me feel so good, this puts a smile on my face for the rest of the day! But after a while, the ponytails blow out like two big puffs.

We call Mama Hattie's mama, Grandma Pearl. She is all of our grandma. Grandma Pearl is very wise and loving. She makes the best chocolate and caramel cakes in the whole wide world! I love it when she lets me take a sip of her coffee from the saucer.

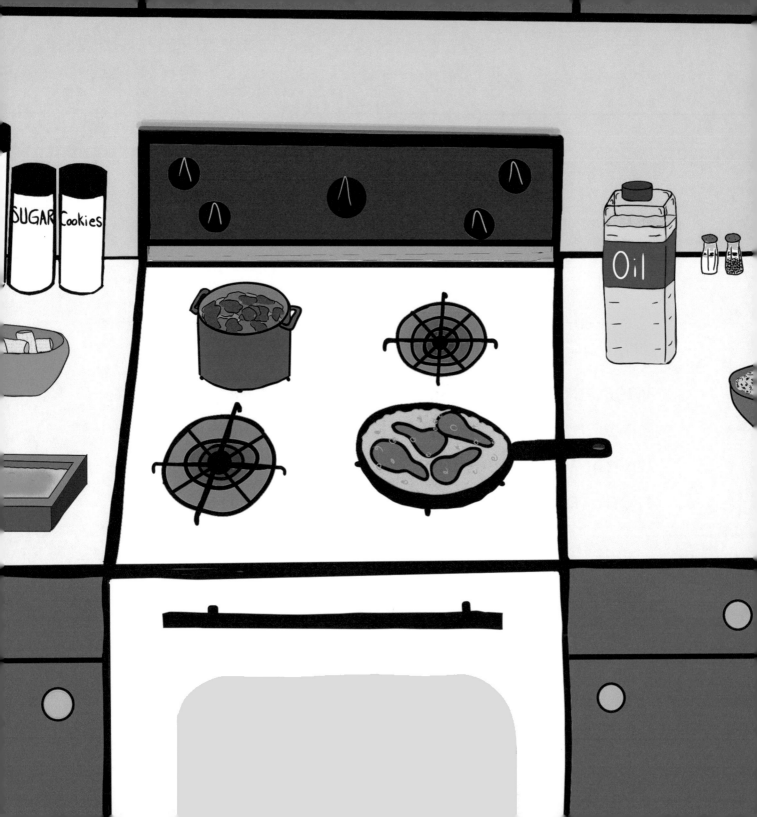

We call my auntie, Auntie Martha or sometimes, just Auntie. She is shorter than my Mama Hattie. She loves to cook. Auntie knows how to cook everything really, really good! She cooks breakfast and dinner for all of us.

25

My sister, Tennie, is tall and skinny and sassy too. She has wavy curly hair. I like to watch her comb her hair. She loves to look in the mirror at herself and make smiling faces. Tennie is very smart, she knows everything! Whatever you want to know, she has the answer.

My niece, Little T is as cute as she can be. She always has a bright smile with her big eyes with long pretty eyelashes. Little T loves to play with paper dolls on the floor. She cuts them out of the Sears book. She is the little sister I always wanted!

29

My brothers, Doc and Doug not forgetting my cousins Ju Ju and Tommy Lee, all of them, are always into mischief. Steve is the youngest brother; he behaves and does not get in trouble like the others. They are all best friends. They have built their own play city under the house. They play all day in their own world. Getting dirty does not bother them.

You might think our home is a little crowded, but we do not notice it at all. We share enough love to go around the house for all of us. We are like brothers and sisters. Some people think we are all sisters and brothers, and we are to me.

33

I see Auntie is in the kitchen cooking dinner. I cannot believe Tennie is helping her cook! Mmmh the food sure smells good! I smell fried chicken; I do not know what else. Everybody is waiting for Auntie to call all of us to the table to eat. We each have our own chair to sit in at the table.

Today is Saturday, it is the middle of the day and it's getting darker outside. I cannot see the big fluffy clouds anymore. The sun is going behind the clouds. The sun was out shining bright earlier today. Now the bright blue sky is turning gray. I have finished my chores. The floors are swept. I have gotten the clothes off of the clothesline outside. I folded them neatly the way Mama Hattie taught me.

Another one of my jobs is to look after Little T. She plays alone and make-believes with her toys. She is on the floor playing with her baby dolls and Tea set. Little T. is having so much fun cutting out paper dolls from the Sears book. Oh my, paper is everywhere! Another job for me.

While watching Little T, I am sitting looking outside the bedroom window. After a while, everything going on around me fades away as I look up at the sky. The clouds are not white and fluffy like cotton balls anymore. They are a darker gray with shapes of mountain tops hanging so low you can touch them.

41

The boys are still under the house. They are shooting marbles now. I can hear them laughing. They are having so much fun! Sometimes I crawl under there to see what they are doing. I don't go too far or stay too long. There might be bugs under there and too much dirt for me.

The rain begins to fall slowly, one drop at a time. I can hear the drops hitting the rooftop. It sounds like tiny rocks pouring from the sky. Oh my, we have a leak! Oh no, there are more leaks! All of us know to put large and small pots out to catch the rain sneaking through the rooftop.

45

Suddenly I hear a deep roaring sound coming from the sky. Then it happens again and again! Out of nowhere, two very bright lights flashed across my eyes. The rain is falling, I can hear it falling harder and harder and the sky is getting darker and darker.

47

Then, I hear a sweet soft voice. Grandma Pearl calls, "Come, come here all of you children!" Grandma Pearl calls all of us to come to her sitting room. Her sitting room is also her bedroom. She is slowly rocking back and forth in her rocking chair while knitting something pretty. "It is time to be quiet and listen as the Lord does His work", said Grandma Pearl.

49.

You see, whenever Grandma Pearl talks to us, we all listen and do as she asks. Grandma Pearl moves her hands as she talks, making motions as if she were drawing a picture for us to see her words. She softly tells us about the goodness of the Lord and how he loves each of us and will take care of us. She is the greatest storyteller ever!

Then, Grandma Pearl begins to hum old gospel songs softly. We all look at her and listen with smiles of peace on our faces. No matter how hard it rains, how loud the thunder roars, or how bright the lighting strikes, we all feel safe and have peace in our home.

53

Before I know it, my eyes are closed. I am resting on the side of my face with my hands folded. I am listening, listening to every word Grandma Pearl says and every hum she makes and gradually falling asleep.

Now I am dreaming. I am Pearlie … I Dream!

55

My heart has that happy feeling again. I feel all warm and nice inside. For some reason, I know that I am dreaming, but I am getting sleepy now. A big yawn… then I fall into a deep sleep, wake up and I am home again.

THE END

Pencil and paper needed. Please do not write in your book. The answers to the questions <u>are not</u> included on this page.

Say It, Hear It, See It, Spell It, Read It, and Write It

1. What is the main idea of the story?

2. Who is the main character in this story?

3. What street did she and her family live on?

4. How many brothers did she have? Write their names.

5. Who did all the children love to listen to?

6. Find five (5) words you want to learn, say and write each word five times each. Then, write a sentence using each word.

Pencil and paper needed. Please do not write in your book. On this page the answers to the questions <u>are included</u> in number 1-5.

Say It, Hear It, See It, Spell It, Read It, and Write It

1. What is the main idea of the story? Simple living and love of family. Learning to listen to learn.

2. Who is the main character in this story? Pearlie

3. What street did she and her family live on? Long Street

4. How many brothers did she have? Three (3). Write their names.

5. Who did all the children love to listen to? Grandma Pearl

6. Find five (5) words you want to learn, say and spell orally while writing each word five times each. Then, write a sentence using each word. Underline the word in each sentence.

About the Author

Yvonne Bardwell Cox and her husband Pastor Tommy L. Cox reside in Columbus, Mississippi. She has a blended family of three handsome sons, three beautiful daughters, eight adorable grandchildren, and two beloved great grandchildren. She is a proud alumnus... successfully completed educational degree status to obtain a Bachelor's in Special Education (Jackson State University, Jackson, MS), Master's and an Educational Specialist in Administration and Supervision (Mississippi State University, Starkville, MS). She is a lifetime professional educator and learner, who believes in securing educational opportunities for all children. A retired Director (Special Education, Gifted Education and 504 Services), Education Consultant, and current School Board member. She has a broad array of teaching and administrative experiences. Having worked in school districts throughout (Mississippi, Georgia, and Tennessee), her desire to author children's books is a lifetime dream come true.

"When you prepare for your future, you prepare your legacy."
Yvonne Bardwell Cox

About the Illustrator

Stacy Johnson is a creative and multi-talented artist currently residing in Tennessee with her husband Michael K. Johnson. At the age of fifteen she discovered her love for the arts, mentored by a family-owned production company called "Joy Art Music - JAM". During this time, she was offered numerous opportunities to express herself through writings, illustrating, creative art design, and music. She discovered an infinite love and gift for many aspects of artistic expression. Stacy studied at the Art Institute of Los Angeles, CA majoring in Interior Design. She is presently refining her skills as a Musical performer and Art Illustrator.

"Big world, little you, both great!"
Stacy Johnson

Printed in the United States
by Baker & Taylor Publisher Services